THREE
EXTRAORDINARY
AMBASSADORS

THIS IS THE FIFTEENTH OF THE
WALTER NEURATH MEMORIAL LECTURES
WHICH ARE GIVEN ANNUALLY EACH SPRING ON
SUBJECTS REFLECTING THE INTERESTS OF
THE FOUNDER
OF THAMES AND HUDSON

THE DIRECTORS WISH TO EXPRESS
PARTICULAR GRATITUDE TO THE GOVERNORS AND
MASTER OF BIRKBECK COLLEGE
UNIVERSITY OF LONDON
FOR THEIR GRACIOUS SPONSORSHIP OF
THESE LECTURES

THREE
EXTRAORDINARY
AMBASSADORS

HAROLD ACTON

THAMES AND HUDSON

Text filmset by Keyspools Ltd, Golborne, Lancs
Printed and bound in Great Britain by Balding & Mansell Ltd, Wisbech

As an Anglo-Florentine I felt greatly honoured by the invitation to add my tribute to the distinguished series of Walter Neurath Memorial lectures. Walter Neurath was pre-eminent among publishers as an ambassador-at-large of the visual arts, and as a citizen of the world who has enriched our knowledge and stimulated our understanding with his creative imagination. So it seemed appropriate to devote this memorial lecture to three British ambassadors to Venice, Florence, and Naples respectively, who exerted an influence on artistic taste in England — Sir Henry Wotton by his 'Elements of Architecture' and Provostship of Eton College; Sir Horace Mann by his patronage of British artists in Italy and his extensive correspondence with dilettanti; and Sir William Hamilton by his pioneering collection which laid the foundation for the Department of Classical Antiquities in the British Museum, apart from his magnificent volumes on the Volcanoes of the Two Sicilies.

The spiritual heritage of Walter Neurath gathers strength from the firm he founded, whose life-enhancing currents continue to flow from the Thames to the Hudson.

1 A panoramic view of Venice in the 17th century by Odoardo Fialetti which Sir
Henry Wotton left to Eton College in his will.

PHILOSOPHEMVR

2 A portrait of Sir Henry Wotton, presumably commissioned while he was Provost at Eton College towards the end of his career.

DURING the centuries before Italy was united, British relations with the Italian States were eminently cultural, and it may be of value to consider an exceptional trio of ambassadors who exerted a greater influence on artistic taste in England than their successors in the British Foreign Service – namely Sir Henry Wotton, Sir Horace Mann, and Sir William Hamilton.

The first two were bachelors; the third was overshadowed by the notoriety of Emma, his second wife. All three became Italianate Englishmen, whose personalities were polished by Venice, Florence, and Naples respectively.

Sir Henry Wotton, the most notable as a linguist, poet and scholar, is still quoted for what he called 'my old merry definition of an ambassador,' which got him into trouble with his master James I: 'An ambassador is an honest man sent to lie abroad for the good of his country.' In his case, as in that of Sir Horace Mann, it would be more exact to say that he was sent to spy abroad, especially on the English Catholics suspected of plotting against King James. The Jesuits were his favourite quarry: he caused their letters to be intercepted and, as he told the Secretary of State Lord Salisbury, 'I must confess myself to have a special appetite to the packets that pass to and from these holy Fathers.' Such a vacillating monarch as James I afforded him little chance to shine in diplomacy, and his missions to Savoy and the Netherlands were unsuccessful, but he was a pioneer in promoting Anglo-Italian relations in the late Tudor and early Stuart periods.

Born on 30 March 1568 at Boughton Malherbe (or Bocton) in the middle of Kent, of an old family of country squires, Wotton liked to consider himself 'a plain Kentish man', but he was quite a match for the wily Venetians with whom he had to deal over a couple of decades. At Oxford he was a boon companion of the many faceted poet John Donne and a pupil of Alberico Gentili, a Protestant refugee who became Professor of Civil Law at the university. Gentili encouraged what Izaak Walton, Wotton's first biographer, described as 'his propensity and connaturalness to the Italian language'. Inspired by Tasso's *Gerusalemme Liberata*, he wrote a play called *Tancredi* which enjoyed contemporary acclaim though its text has been lost. Precociously fluent in Italian, he decided to follow the same career as his elder half-brother Sir Edward, then ambassador in Paris. For six years, from 1589 to 1594, he travelled extensively in Europe, stopping at Heidelberg to perfect his knowledge of German, thence to Altdorf, Ingolstadt, Vienna, Venice, Rome, and Naples. In the latter cities he disguised himself effectively as a German, wearing 'a mighty blue feather in a black cap', carousing and collecting political news for his friend Lord Zouche, always bearing in mind the advice of Scipione Alberti, his Sienese host: '*I pensieri stretti e il viso sciolto*' – your thoughts close and your countenance loose, as he translated it. In Calvinistic Geneva, which gave him a nostalgia for voluptuous Italy, he was the guest of the pioneering classical scholar Isaac Casaubon, from whom he learned Greek as well as French.

After his return to England in 1594 he entered the service of the Earl of Essex, most reckless of royal favourites, as a secretary or agent, joining his expeditions to Cadiz and the Azores and, finally, his ill-fated campaign in Ireland. Before his trial and execution (25 February 1601), Essex advised him to go to Florence with a letter of recommendation to the Medici Grand Duke Ferdinando I. Wotton reached Florence on 4 March 1601, where he made a good impression on the Grand Duke, a former cardinal steeped in Roman and Spanish politics, and it is a curious fact that Wotton owed his début in diplomacy to a Medici.

While the aged Queen Elizabeth was failing, Ferdinando got wind of a plot to poison her presumptive heir James VI of Scotland. Dreading further Spanish expansion, he chose Wotton as his secret envoy to James with a friendly warning and a casket of antidotes. Disguised as Ottavio Baldi, an Italian, Wotton travelled to Scotland by way of Denmark, a rough and hazardous journey. The result was like a scene in an Elizabethan comedy. Asked to lay aside his long rapier, as Izaak Walton relates, he was admitted to the royal presence, and the King 'bade him be bold and deliver his message, for he would undertake for the secrecy of all that were present. Then did Ottavio Baldi deliver his letter and his message to the King in Italian; which when the King had

3 Robert Devereux, 2nd Earl of
Essex, c. 1596.

4 King James I, detail from a
contemporary engraving.

graciously received, after a little pause, Ottavio Baldi steps to the table,
and whispers to the King in his own language that he was an English
man beseeching him for a more private conference with His Majesty,
and that he might be concealed during his stay in that nation, which was
promised, and really performed by the King . . .'

During the three months Wotton spent in rugged Scotland, he
charmed the King with his brilliant conversation, and he returned to the
court of Tuscany with enhanced prestige. When James became King of
England he knighted Wotton and sent him as ambassador to Venice. In
Venice, still the chief exchange mart between East and West, he was to
live intermittently for the next twenty years (1604–10; 1616–19;
1621–23).

Threatened by Spanish encirclement, the Venetian Republic looked
to England and France for support. Consequently Wotton was
welcomed by the Doge and Council of twenty-five senators, whom he

addressed with a florid eulogy of their ancient institutions. But in some ways his position resembled that of an ambassador behind the Iron Curtain today, for no Venetian official could associate privately with a foreign envoy under penalties of life imprisonment or death. Apart from his colleagues there was a large community of British students at Padua University, and he was allowed to keep a chaplain in the embassy. Wotton commuted between a luxurious palace at Canareggio (near the present railway station) and a villa at Noventa on the Brenta canal in summer, surrounded by congenial scholars with whom he played bowls and billiards for relaxation. He was extremely musical, with a preference for the viola de gamba. During his second embassy he rented the more central Palazzo Gussoni on the Grand Canal.

After the Earl of Arundel, Wotton was one of the first collectors of Venetian paintings, not only for himself but for Lord Salisbury and the

5, 6 Doge Leonardo Donato giving audience to Sir Henry Wotton, painting by Odoardo Fialetti; and a detail showing Wotton seated on the Doge's right.

Duke of Buckingham, and he employed the enterprising agent Daniel Nys to hunt for works of art. He ordered a copy in mosaics of a portrait of Lord Salisbury which still exists at Hatfield. Jacopo Palma il Giovane, Leandro Bassano, and Alessandro Varotari, il Padovanino, were still alive and active: their names crop up among Wotton's purchases for Salisbury and Buckingham. Like later ambassadors in Italy he kept open house for English visitors in the early days of the Grand Tour.

Besides settling trade disputes and negotiating for the suppression of piracy – the Adriatic was infested with British buccaneers – Wotton's predominant aim was to promote an anti-papal league of Protestant states. The Pope having quarrelled with the Republic about their imprisonment of two priests, Wotton fanned the flame with gusto. A new Doge, Leonardo Donato, confronted the new Pope Paul V when he issued a bull of interdict and excommunication against the Republic. The Servite friar, Paolo Sarpi, historian of the Council of Trent, persuaded the Senate to resist the interdict and the clergy to continue their functions. A face-saving solution was found by Henry IV of France: the priests were delivered to the French ambassador 'without prejudice to the Republic's future rights to try such persons', and the

7 Robert Cecil, 1st Earl of Salisbury, detail of a mosaic portrait.

8 George Villiers, 1st Duke of Buckingham, detail of a portrait *c*. 1616.

9 Paolo Sarpi, theologian and historian of the Council of Trent, detail of a portrait.

ambassador handed them over to the French Cardinal de Joyeuse as the Pope's representative. Venice's resistance to the interdict encouraged Wotton to believe that it was ripe for conversion to Protestantism, but the Venetians were more patriotic than devout and Sarpi, their official theologian and canonist, was a reformer mainly opposed to the Pope's temporal power. Wotton had a boundless esteem for Sarpi, whom he met secretly through his chaplain William Bedell, an ardent evangelist. His Anglican zeal often outran his discretion, as when he resigned in a rage because King James's tactless effusion, *The Premonition to all Most Mighty Monarchs, Kings, Free Princes, and States of Christendom*, translated into Italian by Bedell, was banned in Venice. The Doge, who had no desire to antagonize an ally, sent a special envoy to placate the King, and his petulant ambassador was excused. In his farewell audience after Wotton's first embassy the Doge declared: 'It is much to your praise and a matter of no small wonder, that although there was in your house another religion, yet both you and all your suite have acted so prudently and circumspectly that not a breath of scandal has touched you.'

Wotton's two other diplomatic missions to Venice were less eventful except for a quarrel with Lady Arundel, to whom he had to apologize

An Aire of a Canzo, composed in honour of the most illustrious Princesse
the Lady *Elizabeth, &c.*

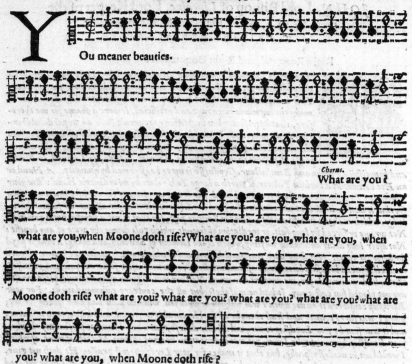

Y Ou meaner beauties.

Chorus.
What are you?

what are you, when Moone doth rise? What are you? are you, what are you, when

Moone doth rise? what are you? what are you? what are you? what are you? what are

you? what are you, when Moone doth rise?

2 You Violets, which first appeare,
By those your purple mantles knowne,
Much like proud Virgins of the yeare,
As if the Spring were all your owne,
What are you when Rose is blowne?

3 You wandring chanters of the Wood,
Who fill the eares with Natures layes,
Thinking your passions vnderstood,
By weaker accents, What's your praise
When Philomel her voice doth raise?

4 So when my Princesse shall be seene,
In sweetnesse of her lookes and minde,
By vertue first, then choyse a Queene,
O tell if she were not design'd,
Th'Eclipse and glory of her kinde?

10, 11 A poem by Henry Wotton to Elisabeth, Queen of Bohemia, set to music in the early 17th century; and a portrait of Elisabeth by Gerard Honthorst, 1642.

in the Doge's presence. (Rumour had associated her with Antonio Foscarini, the former Venetian ambassador executed for a false accusation of treason, and Wotton sent her word that she was not *persona grata* in the Republic. The indignant countess had insisted on a public apology.) His later correspondence was filled with details of the Spanish plot to overthrow the government, which was dramatized in Otway's tragedy *Venice Preserved*.

Wotton was certainly the first Englishman to collect Palladian drawings and his little book on *The Elements of Architecture* (1624) was his enduring tribute to the Venice he loved. Sir Reginald Blomfield described him as 'the first English writer to attempt a practical manual of architecture; and, on the whole, and within his very limited scope, he succeeded better in his attempt than any subsequent writer.' The serene solemnity of Palladio's greatest church, Il Redentore, was his architectural ideal. Ruskin dismissed it as 'small and contemptible', if not as 'barbarous' as San Giorgio Maggiore, whereas Wotton wrote that pointed arches 'ought to be exiled from judicious eyes, and left to their first inventors, the Goths or Lombards, amongst other reliques of that barbarous age.' That secret harmony of the proportions which he called

'Eurythmia' was what Wotton most admired in Palladian buildings. He belonged to the late Renaissance.

As his leading biographer Logan Pearsall Smith pointed out, Wotton was 'the best letter-writer of his time — the first Englishman whose correspondence deserves to be read for its literary quality, apart from its historical interest.' Of his surviving poems, the lyric 'On his Mistress, the Queen of Bohemia' and 'The Character of a Happy Life' are deservedly famous. That happiness he was to achieve as Provost of Eton, 'the college being to his mind,' to quote Walton, 'as a quiet harbour to a sea-faring man after a tempestuous voyage.'

He died peacefully at Eton in his seventy-second year on 5 December, 1639. In the previous decade his agent Daniel Nys had purchased the great Mantua collection for Charles I, who evidently had a high opinion of Wotton's expertise, for he summoned him to Whitehall to pronounce judgment on some newly arrived pictures in 1631. A passage in the second part of his *Elements of Architecture* shows that in his appreciation of painting and sculpture he was well in advance of his age. To paraphrase this in modern language, he considered that the artist whose chief aim was to imitate nature could be too natural, and that excessive fidelity to visual appearance or ideal forms resulted in loss of beauty. For instance Dürer did too much express *'that which was'*, and Michelangelo *'that which should be'*.

It was ultimately due to Wotton that Palladio gained so many devotees in England, from Inigo Jones to the post-Restoration. If his pamphlet, as he modestly called it, exerted an influence out of all proportion to its length, his Provostship of Eton during the fifteen years between the accession of Charles I and the approaching Civil War ranked with those of Sir Henry Savile and the latterday M. R. James. 'He was pleased constantly,' as Izaak Walton wrote, 'to breed up one or more hopeful youths, which he picked out of the school, and took into his own domestic care, and to attend him at meals.' Among these were two sons of his Irish friend the Earl of Cork, Francis, Viscount Shannon, and Robert Boyle the future scientist, who was to describe him as 'a person who was not only a fine gentleman himself, but very well skilled in the art of making others so.'

18

12 Eton College Chapel, the Provost's Lodge, and Windsor Castle, *c.* 1600.

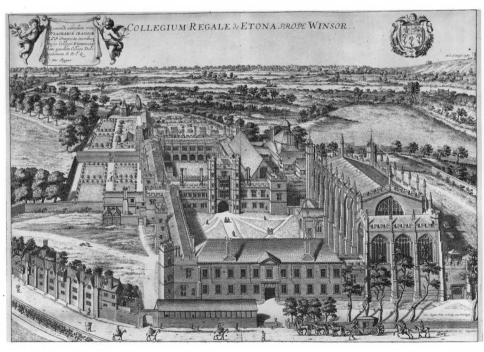

13 A view of Eton College in an engraving of 1688.

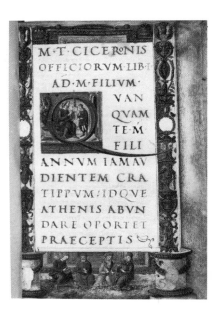

14 A page from a 15th-century manuscript of Cicero's *De Officiis*, which was given to Eton College by Wotton.

15 A letter in Wotton's handwriting dated 11 March 1619.

He was ordained a deacon in 1627 and spent his mornings in meditation with the Bible, but after dinner 'nothing but cheerful thoughts possessed his mind,' for 'he was a great lover of his neighbours, and a bountiful entertainer of them very often at his table, where his meat was choice, and his discourse better.' He shared Izaak Walton's 'innate pleasure of angling, which he would usually call *his idle time, not idly spent*: saying often he would rather live five *May months*, than *forty Decembers*.' Before John Milton's Italian journey he presented Wotton with a copy of *Comus*. In his letter of thanks Wotton wrote: 'I should much commend the tragical part, if the lyrical did not ravish me with a certain Dorique delicacy in your songs and odes; whereunto I must plainly confess to have seen yet nothing parallel in our language . . .' That Milton valued his criticism is proved by his printing it in the 1645 edition of his collected poems.

The long catalogue of bequests in Wotton's will illustrates the variety of his interests. These included four portraits of Venetian Doges by Odoardo Fialetti, a pupil of Tintoretto, and a picture of 'the Venetian College, where Ambassadors had their audience, done by the same hand'; another Doge attributed to Titian; 'the Four Seasons of Old Bassano', bought in Venice, with instructions to hang them 'near the eye', besides 'my great Loadstone; and a piece of Amber ... which is thought somewhat rare; a piece of Crystal Sexangular ... grasping several things within it, which I bought in the Rhaetian Alps'; and 'my Viol di Gamba, which hath been twice in Italy'; finally, 'to the Library of Eaton College [sic] I leave all my manuscripts not before disposed, and to each of the Fellows a plain ring of gold, enamelled black, all save the verge, with this Motto within, *Amor vincit omnia*.'

22

16 A view of Florence in the 18th century by Thomas Patch, which was in Horace Walpole's collection.

17 Sir Horace Mann, a portrait by John Astley, 1752.

Almost a century after Wotton's death the Prime Minister Sir Robert Walpole appointed young Horace Mann, a distant kinsman, to the English Legation in Florence. There he remained for the next forty-eight years, until his death in 1786. His duties were similar to Wotton's, protecting British interests in general, residents and travellers in particular. The latter were far more numerous and sophisticated than in Wotton's day. But whereas Wotton, obsessed by the Gunpowder Plot, had to keep an eye on British Papists and exiles, Mann had to watch the Stuart Pretenders and Jacobite expatriates. He did this conscientiously, as we know from his voluminous letters to Horace Walpole, Sir Robert's youngest son, but he was also an accomplished diplomat with an intimate knowledge of Florentine society.

Horace Walpole, eleven years younger than Mann, was twenty-three when he came to Florence with the poet Thomas Gray in December 1739, and except for an interval of three months he stayed with Mann for over a year – until 25 April 1741. From Rosalba Carriera's portrait of him, we may judge his appearance at that period, a bright-eyed youth with a feminine cast of features. He entered too zestfully into the Carnival spirit to please his contemplative companion, and became the *cicisbeo*, or accepted gallant, of Marchesa Grifoni, who presented him with a lapdog called Patapan when he left for England. Though he never returned to Florence he corresponded with Mann for the next forty-five years, during which they never met. Considering the enormous bulk and variety of his literary productions the high quality of his letters is amazing. Macaulay described him as 'the most Frenchified English writer of the eighteenth century', but he granted that 'no man who has written so much is so seldom tiresome.'

Mann's style, on the other hand, was progressively Italianate, as if his English had rusted. His letters provide a detailed panorama of eighteenth-century Florence and Anglo-Italian relations. 'I consider your friendship as a treasure inestimable,' he told the younger Horace. 'I cannot conceive how 'tis possible for anyone to get so much news as you do the instant you arrive in a place. How extremely good you are to write to me. Your letters make me infinitely happy. I can send you nothing in return but what's very trifling. Our countrymen, I find, will in all parts be most supremely ridiculous.' And the younger Horace exclaimed: 'We are the Orestes and Pylades of letter-writing.'*

Although Mann's salary and allowances were often in arrears he occupied a spacious mansion, the Casa Manetti in Via S. Spirito, and kept a guest-house, the Casa Ambrogi, for privileged visitors. The ground floor of Casa Manetti he described as 'the prettiest apartment you can imagine ... very genteel and vastly gay'. He told Walpole (12 August 1741) that he rose at 7.30 a.m., ate very moderately at dinner 'of a very odd dish, lamb's brains, about four or five ounces, soup, and stewed peaches. I return to bed at 2.30 p.m.; at about 6.30 p.m. I drink tea for the sake of the bread and butter I eat with it. This is performed under the orange trees where I am now sitting to write. I receive company in the garden and am famous for the best lemonade in Florence.' His assemblies in the garden were 'vastly resorted to'; in winter his Thursday nights were 'vastly gay'. Usually the ladies numbered eighty, 'the men out of all proportion, even of three to one, which is the common calculation.' Occasionally a couple caused scandal by their brazenly amorous behaviour, since 'love you know is the chief employment in this country.' But 'Oh, the number of English! I am absolutely ruined in feasting them ... hundreds who only come to scramble for sherbets and to pocket the glasses.'

Mann's salary, even when paid, would not have sufficed for so much hospitality, had he not obtained commissions for the works of art and other luxuries he procured. These ranged between 'a prodigious fine head by Guido [Reni] allowed by everybody to be his first and best manner' and demijohns of orange flower water of the finest sort, double distilled from Malta (reputed to help digestion, refresh the heart and brain, and promote the menses). He was also asked to procure melon seeds and Maltese cats, 'the largest male and female that can be got.'

---

* Fortunately their vast correspondence has been preserved, superbly edited by W. S. Lewis, Warren Hunting Smith, and George L. Lam, Oxford 1961.

18 Horace Walpole, 4th Earl of Orford, a portrait by Rosalba Carriera, 1741.

19–21 Sir Horace Mann's house in
Florence, Casa Manetti (left), and
two paintings by Thomas Patch of
parties in the house.

Horace Walpole applied to him frequently for some painting or decorative trinket that had caught his fancy. Thus in November 1741: 'I will trouble you with a new commission: I find I cannot live without Stosch's intaglio of the gladiator with the vase, upon a granite. You know I offered him fifty pounds: I think rather than not have it, I would give an hundred . . . perhaps he would part with his Meleager too. You see I am as eager about baubles as if I were going to Louis [Siries, the dealer] at the Palazzo Vecchio! You can't think what a closet I have fitted up! Such a mixture of French gaiety and Roman *virtù*! You would be in love with it: I have not rested till it was finished: I long to have you see it! Now I am angry that I did not buy the Hermaphrodite; the man would have sold it for 25 sequins [£12.50]: do buy it for me . . .' (Baron Philipp von Stosch was the disreputable virtuoso-cum-dealer who was paid to spy on the Stuart Pretender.)

Again, 18 March 1756, he wrote: 'I must now give you a new commission, and for no less a minister than the Chancellor of the

Exchequer: Sir George Lyttleton desires you will send him for his hall [Hagley Hall, Worcestershire] the gesses of the Venus, the dancing faun, the Apollo Medicis, (I think there is a cast of it), the Mercury, and some other female statue, at your choice; he desires besides three pairs of Volterra vases of the size to place on tables, and different patterns.' Previously he had asked for 'four of the Volterra urns of the chimney-piece size' on behalf of Sir Francis Dashwood, that profligate member of the Dilettanti Society who was depicted by George Knapton as a Franciscan friar holding a chalice and leering at the middle of a marble Venus.

While still in quest of important additions to his father's collection Walpole wrote: 'I was mentioning to Sir Robert some pictures in Italy which I wished him to buy: two particularly, if they can be got, would make him delight in you beyond measure. They are a Madonna and Child by Domenichino in the palace Zambeccari at Bologna ... The other is by Correggio, in a convent at Parma, and reckoned the best of that hand in the world. There are the Madonna and Child, St Catherine, St Matthew and other figures; 'tis a most known picture, and has been engraved by Augustin Carracci. If you can employ anybody privately to inquire about these pictures, be so good as to let me know: Sir Robert would not scruple almost any price, for he has of neither hand.'

Mann succeeded in obtaining the Domenichino, which was eventually sold with the rest of the Houghton collection to Catherine II of Russia, and hung in the Hermitage at St Petersburg where it was attributed to Sassoferrato. The Correggio was bought by the Duke of Parma and is now in the gallery there.

Mann could not afford such treasures for himself, but his rooms were filled with copies of masterpieces he admired, and he also obtained replicas for such clients as the Earl of Northumberland. Sir Horace, as he became, could never compete with Consul Joseph Smith in Venice, who was more of an art dealer than a consul. Mann had to be satisfied with the products of the English artists who called on him: his large reception room contained four harbour scenes by Thomas Patch. This versatile artist had studied in Rome under Claude-Joseph Vernet, but

30

22, 23 An engraving of Meleager and Atalanta from Stosch's *Gemmae Antiquae*, 1724; and one of the Madonna and Child attributed in the 18th century to Domenichino, but now believed to be by Sassoferrato.

after being expelled for his sexual aberrations he settled in Florence, across the street from Casa Manetti. Sir Horace winked at his morals and encouraged his art. Besides his views of the city there was a vogue for his painted caricatures. Mann wrote that young Englishmen often employed him 'to make conversation pieces of any number, for which they then draw lots; but Patch is so prudent as never to caricature anybody without his consent and a full liberty to exert his talents.' His charges were modest: about £8 for a caricature group of four figures and about £6 for a Florentine landscape, usually derived from a Zocchi engraving.

An outstanding example of his caricature groups was recently discovered as a screen by Mr Brinsley Ford, who restored it to its original form. This represents *A Gathering of Dilettanti round the Medici Venus*, containing twenty-five figures: of these only Sir Horace Mann, the opulent Lord Cowper, *doyen* of the British colony, and Patch himself, measuring the Medici Venus, have been identified.

24 Thomas Patch's painting of a gathering of Dilettanti around the Medici Venus, 1760–70. This includes Patch, centre, on the steps, measuring the Medici Venus;

Sir Horace Mann, in left background, his head in front of the statue of Mercury; and
Lord Cowper, second from right.

25, 26 Zoffany's painting of the Tribuna; and a detail showing Patch, holding the *Venus of Urbino*, and Mann, with the star.

Inevitably Mr Ford's painting recalls Zoffany's overcrowded *Tribuna*, which was painted for George III between 1772 and 1778. The Grand Duke Peter Leopold allowed Zoffany to move seven masterpieces from the Pitti Palace into the Uffizi for the occasion. These were reproduced with photographic precision, but Zoffany also included a swarm of English residents and tourists peering at the famous works of art. Sir Horace stands in the foreground, wearing the ribbon and star of the Order of the Bath, and he wrote to the other Horace: 'He [Zoffany] told me that the King had expressly ordered my portrait to be there, which I did not believe, but did not object to it; but he made the same merit with all the young travellers then in Florence, some of whom he afterwards

27 Three figures from a fresco in
the Brancacci Chapel, S. Maria del
Carmine, engraved (in reverse) by
Patch for his book, *Life of Masaccio*.
These figures survive and are now
attributed to Filippino Lippi.

28 The baptistery doors in
Florence, a page from Patch's book
of engravings, 1774.

rubbed out.' Walpole replied: 'The first thing I looked for was *you*, and
I could not find you. "Pray, who is that Knight of the Bath?" – "Sir
Horace Mann." – "Impossible," said I. My dear Sir, how you have left
me in the lurch! You are grown fat, jolly, young, while I am become the
skeleton of Methuselah.' Though he was impressed by its meticulous
detail he thought Zoffany might have been better employed: 'His talent
is representing natural humour. I look upon him as a Dutch painter
polished or civilized.'

Thomas Patch was also included in Zoffany's *Tribuna*, and if we
combine that group of stylish figures (how unlike our modern tourists in
khaki shorts and blue jeans) with Patch's caricatures, we get a visual
conflation of Mann's gossipy letters, even though the ladies are absent.
Mann wrote of Patch, 'he is really a genius', but he is of greater historical
interest for his engravings of Giotto's and Masaccio's frescoes in the
church of S. Maria del Carmine before most of it was destroyed by fire in
1771. These were published in 1772, together with twenty-four
engravings from Fra Bartolommeo's paintings in San Marco, dedicated
to both Horaces Mann and Walpole. Patch also published an illustrated
account of Ghiberti's doors of the Florentine Baptistery in 1774, the

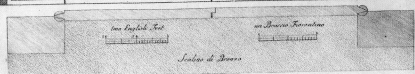

two English Feet   un Braccio Fiorentino

Scalino di Bronzo

ELEVATION AND PLAN OF THE GATE OF S.ᵗ IOHN   Alzata e Pianta della Porta di S. Giovanni

engravings so arranged that 'the impressions may be joined together to form an exact half of the gate.'*

Among other English artists patronized by Mann the brothers Enrico and Ignazio Hugford were exceptional, having been born in Italy. Enrico, a Benedictine monk, became Abbot of Vallombrosa; he also invented a special technique for producing decorative pictures and table-tops in scagliola as a hobby, and these were much sought after, as we learn from Mann's correspondence. Ignazio was a pupil of the prolific baroque painter Anton Domenico Gabbiani, yet he had a taste then singular for collecting Tuscan primitives. A successful dealer, on friendly terms with Sir Joshua Reynolds, Gavin Hamilton, and the sculptor Joseph Wilton, who stayed with him, Ignazio Hugford was also suspected of producing clever fakes. He published the sixth edition of Vasari's *Lives*, and over 3,000 drawings in the Uffizi were formerly in his collection.

Mann's activities as envoy extraordinary and plenipotentiary were less strenuous after the failure of the Jacobite rebellion and the Peace of Aix-la-Chapelle in 1748, and his letters continued to chronicle the minutiae of the Tuscan Court and the matrimonial misadventures of the Count of Albany, Prince Charles Edward Stuart. But his physique, which Walpole compared to wet brown paper, was far from robust, and the ceremonial of the Court exhausted him. His last letters were written with a gouty tremulous hand, unless dictated. He died on 16 November 1786 at the age of eighty. In February of that year he had written to Walpole: 'Though I am not vehemently attached to this world, I must do it the justice to own that I have no right to complain of my lot in it, during a very decent course of time, and with more comfort than I had any pretensions to, at the beginning of it. Upon the whole, therefore, I am perfectly well satisfied, and look forward with a total indifference as to myself, though to the last hour of my existence, I shall be anxious to hear of your welfare.'

---

* A curious forerunner of Mr David Finn's publication, *The Florence Baptistery Doors*, photographs by David Finn, introduction by Kenneth Clark, London/New York 1980.

29 A landscape in scagliola by Enrico Hugford.

30 A view of Naples from Sir William Hamilton's book *Campi Phlegraei*, 1776–79.

31 Sir William Hamilton, a portrait by David Allan, 1775.

Over twenty years previously Mann had told Walpole that Sir William Hamilton and his first wife 'were cast into Leghorn some days ago by a storm, and very kindly came to make me a visit whilst the wind changed. The poor, good, sickly lady was seized with a fit of the asthma, as soon as she got out of the coach, at my door, and could with difficulty get to her apartment, but it was rather a slight fit and did not last so long as usual, so that she could dine at table the next day. Did not your ears tingle? for we talked of nothing else but you and your Château of Strawberry.'

It is a cruel irony that the most aesthetic of our ambassadors is chiefly remembered as the complacent husband of Lord Nelson's Lady Hamilton. The Cinderella legend of the Cheshire blacksmith's daughter has overshadowed that of her distinguished husband and impresario, who played the rôle of Pygmalion to this Galatea. 'Sir William has actually married his gallery of statues,' was Horace Walpole's comment on his second marriage, and Emma brought his statues to ephemeral life in her 'Attitudes'.

A son of Lord Archibald and grandson of the third Duke of Hamilton, William was thirty-four when he came to Naples as British envoy and plenipotentiary in 1764. Previously he had served ten years in the army during the Seven Years War, as an equerry to the future George III who called him his foster-brother, and as a Member of Parliament until he married Catherine Barlow, an heiress with considerable property in Wales. His delicate, devoted wife was an accomplished musician, and he seems to have grown fond of her though it had been a marriage of convenience. Tall and slender, with an aquiline nose and suave manners, he eventually became as popular an institution in Naples as Sir Horace Mann had been in Florence. He too was surrounded by English artists, and Palazzo Sessa was to become an intellectual and musical centre unique among foreign embassies.

Hamilton was qualified to extract every drop of honey from the huge hive of Naples. Vesuvius beckoned to him with its plume of smoke. He

32–34 Portrait by David Allan of Sir William with the first Lady Hamilton (above). A room in the Palazzo Sessa, and another room showing Sir William with Lord Fortrose and the violinist Pugnani, attributed to Pietro Fabris.

climbed it often, especially when it threatened to erupt. As he was also a keen geologist he described its activities in a series of enthusiastic letters to the Royal Society which have been printed. He rented the Villa Angelica in its vicinity in order not to miss its most dramatic manifestations. Accompanied by a one-eyed local guide, Bartolomeo Pumo, whom he called the Cyclops of Vesuvius, he peered into its mouth, and he often spent the night on its slopes when puffs of smoke appeared 'tinged like clouds with the setting sun.' 'It is impossible to describe the beautiful appearance of the girandoles of red-hot stones, far surpassing the most astonishing fireworks,' he wrote; and when he published two magnificent volumes of his *Campi Phlegraei: Observations on the Volcanos of the Two Sicilies*, he found a congenial artist, Pietro Fabris, English in spite of his name, to illustrate them. Hamilton's friend Sir Joseph Banks, later President of the Royal Society, wrote: 'I read your letters with that kind of fidgety anxiety which continually upbraids me for not being in a similar situation. I envy you; I pity myself.'

35–37 Two illustrations of the famous eruption of Vesuvius on 9 August 1779 ; and (below) a night view of a current of lava on 11 May 1771 showing, among the spectators, Hamilton and the Sicilian King and Queen.

38 View of the first discovery of the Temple of Isis at Pompeii, from *Campi Phlegraei*.

Besides the thrills of Vesuvius there were the excavations at Herculaneum and Pompeii to whet Hamilton's acquisitive appetite. He was the first Englishman to obtain treasures from these buried cities on the spot. He assembled some 750 so-called Etruscan vases, together with 175 terracottas, 300 pieces of ancient glass, 627 bronzes, a quantity of armour, 150 objects in ivory, 150 gems and as many gold articles of jewelry, more than 6,000 coins, mostly from Magna Graecia, which he brought to England in 1772 and sold to the British Museum for £8,400, thus laying the foundation for its Department of Classical Antiquities. His vases were scrupulously catalogued by the romantic French connoisseur Pierre François Hugues, self-styled Baron d'Hancarville, and published in four folio volumes with copious engravings – a production which cost Sir William the then extravagant sum of £6,000. Sir Joshua Reynolds, recently elected the first President of the Royal Academy, wrote to him in 1769 that he admired it exceedingly, and that it would tend 'to the advancement of the arts, as adding more materials for genius to work upon.' Hamilton's desire that his collection should provide models for modern artists and craftsmen was soon

39 Frontispiece from Sir William Hamilton's *Collection of Engravings from Ancient Vases*, 1791–95.

40 A vase painting from the catalogue by P. F. Hugues of Sir William Hamilton's collection of antiquities.

41 The famous Portland Vase.

realized by the master potter Josiah Wedgwood who copied several figures from the folios at his new factory named Etruria.

Having sold one collection he proceeded to form another, most of which was shipwrecked, but the four volumes entitled *A Collection of Engravings from Ancient Vases ... Discovered in the Kingdom of the Two Sicilies*, published between 1791 and 1795, leave us with a clear record of their shapes and designs. Together with the previous folios, they exerted a wide influence on the Neo-Classical movement in England, especially on John Flaxman and Henry Fuseli when they illustrated Homer. Sir William's purchase of the celebrated Portland Vase of blue and white glass in 1783 was equally far-reaching in its effects. Fortunately six plaster copies had been made of it by James Tassie after Pichler's mould, for it was smashed by a drunken vandal in 1845 and pieced together with amazing dexterity by Thomas Doubleday of the British Museum. 'The person I bought it of at Rome,' Hamilton later told Wedgwood, 'will do me the justice to say that the superior excellence of this exquisite masterpiece of ancient art struck me so much at first sight, that I eagerly

42 Sir Joshua Reynolds's painting of a group of members of the Society of Dilettanti. Hamilton is sitting in the centre with his hand on the book.

asked, "Is it yours? Will you sell it to me?" He answered, "Yes, but never under £1000." "I will give you a thousand pounds," I said, and so I did, though God knows it was not very convenient for me at that time, and the business was concluded in a moment.' The third Duke of Portland, whose mother bought it from Hamilton, lent it to Wedgwood for a year to enable him to reproduce it in his jasper ware.

Hunting for antiques, investigating the caprices of Vesuvius, entertaining the constant flow of Grand Tourists, acting as cicerone to visiting Royalty, Hamilton considered that the most strenuous of his unofficial duties was to join the young King's hunting and fishing expeditions in every kind of weather. As his eldest brother was half-witted, Ferdinando's education had been neglected for the sake of his health; he remained a boisterous boy with a lifelong mania for field sports. While Hamilton hobnobbed with the King, his invalid wife stayed at home with her harpsichord, her solitude relieved by random guests such as William Beckford, whose mother was a cousin of Sir William's. Beckford's taste, like Horace Walpole's, was turning

43 Emma, Lady Hamilton, the portrait by George Romney.

44 One of Lady Hamilton's 'attitudes', a contemporary engraving.

towards the Gothic, but music formed a bond with his hostess when he stayed at Caserta in November 1780. 'After my mother you are the person I love best in the universe. I could remain with you all my life listening to your music and your conversation,' he wrote to her. But Beckford was to live till 1844 whereas poor Lady Hamilton died in 1782. Her death ended the calmest period of Sir William's life. Next year he returned to England to bury her, and it was then that he met Emma Hart, the mistress of his nephew Charles Greville.

The sequel is too well known for me to recapitulate here. Greville palmed off his beautiful but inconvenient concubine, aged twenty-one, on his fifty-six-year-old uncle, never expecting them to marry, as they finally did in 1791. Sir William thus added a living work of art to his collection. Many painters have familiarized us with her features, beginning with Romney for whom she had posed when she was kept by Greville in Edgware Row. In Naples she was to pose in various classical rôles for the guests of Palazzo Sessa. Sir William delighted in her *tableaux vivants*, the so-called 'Attitudes', of which Goethe has left a glowing description and Frederick Rehberg an album of engravings.

Though George III granted his permission to the marriage, Queen Charlotte would not receive a bride with so dubious a past. This was a blow to Emma's social ambitions, for it would prevent her from appearing as ambassadress at the Neapolitan Court. On her way back to Naples, however, she was received by the less prudish Marie Antoinette, who entrusted her with a letter to her sister. This gave Emma an opportunity to visit Queen Maria Carolina in private, who realized that she might be useful as an intermediary for secret communications with the British ambassador. These became frequent after France declared war on Great Britain in February 1793 and a treaty with Naples was signed by Hamilton in the same year.

On 11 September Captain Horatio Nelson arrived with dispatches for Sir William: reinforcements were needed in the occupation of Toulon. Sir William invited him to stay at Palazzo Sessa, and an immediate sympathy sprang up between the sixty-three-year-old ambassador and Nelson on the verge of thirty-five. In fact Nelson made a deeper impression on Sir William than on Emma, and if he was susceptible to her beauty then he had more pressing engagements. News of a French corvette off Sardinia prevented him from entertaining the King on board the *Agamemnon*, but he corresponded with Sir William for the next five years.

Queen Maria Carolina's hatred of France became pathological after the execution of her sister in October 1793, but her thirst for vengeance soon overcame her morbid depression. She found relaxation in the naive society of Emma Hamilton, whose head was completely turned by the Queen's condescension. 'I am almost sick of grandeur,' she wrote to her former lover Greville, but her appetite for grandeur grew apace when she fancied she had won the Queen's confidence.

Sir William still found leisure for his collection, and for the third most violent eruption of Vesuvius recorded in history. As if to vie with the French Revolution, Vesuvius blew its top off in June 1794. The neighbouring Mount Somma now rose above it. Sir William sent an eye-witness account of 'this great operation of nature' to the Royal Society as on previous occasions. Torre del Greco was 'overwhelmed, burnt, and destroyed' by torrents of lava which spread towards the sea

45 Horatio Nelson, a portrait by
L. F. Abbott.

46 A bust of Queen Maria Carolina.

and formed a new promontory. Hamilton attempted to approach it by
boat on the morning of 17 June, but the sea was boiling even at a
hundred yards distance, and his hand was scalded when he put it into
the water. The pitch was melting from the bottom of the boat, which
began to leak. Landing near Torre del Greco, he climbed to the top of
one of the highest houses still standing; most of them were buried under
lava, which did not deter the jackal-thieves from looting. 'What drove
me from this melancholy spot,' he wrote, 'was that one of the robbers,
with a great pig on his shoulders, pursued by the proprietor with a long
gun pointing at him, kept dodging me to save himself! I bade him throw
the pig down, which he did, and the proprietor, satisfied with having
recovered his loss, told me there were thieves in every house.'

At the end of June he made his sixty-eighth ascent of the volcano to
which he had devoted so much time and energy over more than thirty
years, attended by his veteran guide Bartolomeo Pumo. The ground was

so hot that his thick-soled boots were burnt through, and they had to retreat from the noxious 'exhalations of sulphurous and vitriolic vapours'.

After Bonaparte's sweeping victories, a peace treaty had reluctantly been signed between Naples and the French, which saved the country from invasion for the time being. Hamilton agreed with Nelson and the Queen that this had been a mistake: the French would break the treaty whenever it suited them. To his old friend Sir Joseph Banks he wrote that his constant agitation and fatigue of mind during the last six years – in fact since he had married Emma – had injured his health: 'I had much rather occupy myself in admiring the wisdom of the Creator in a Bee-hive or a nest of Ants, than turn my eyes towards the glaring folly that seems to direct almost every Government in Europe.'

He was hoping to sell his vase collection – 'more than a thousand vases, and one half of them figured' – for seven thousand pounds sterling to the King of Prussia, who regrettably failed to buy them. On 14 July 1798 James Clark made an inventory of his pictures* – a total of 347 paintings, including the 'laughing boy by Leonardo da Vinci' now attributed to Luini, a Titian, a Rembrandt, a Rubens, a Velazquez, a Van Dyck, two Poussins, several Salvator Rosas and Canalettos, and fourteen portraits of Emma in histrionic poses. Though some of the attributions were fanciful it was an impressive collection for a man of comparatively modest means. Emma had brought him no dowry, but her youthful exuberance was a tonic substitute.

News of Nelson's great victory in Aboukir Bay was the greatest tonic of all. The battered hero, who had lost his right arm and right eye since his last visit to Naples, and had been wounded in the forehead recently, received a spectacular ovation in the most spectacular of cities.

Emma swooned at the sight of him on board the *Vanguard* and nursed him tenderly in Palazzo Sessa, ablaze with three thousand lamps in his honour. Eight hundred guests attended his birthday gala on 29 September, when a rostral column was unveiled with *Veni, vidi, vinci* inscribed with the names of all his captains in the Battle of the Nile.

---

* The manuscript of which is in the Fitzwilliam Museum, Cambridge.

Emma's strident soprano favoured them with the National Anthem to which an extra verse had been added by Miss Cornelia Knight, an admiral's spinster daughter, joining 'great Nelson's name, First on the roll of Fame', to resounding applause. After his prolonged celibacy at sea small wonder he was bowled over by this flamboyant specimen of femininity. As for Hamilton, his intense admiration for Nelson was gratified by the flowering of this new friendship. Henceforth he was to play second fiddle in his marriage. He disagreed with Lord Grenville, the Foreign Secretary, who 'saw no safety in Naples but submission to the French,' and shared Nelson's view that 'the boldest measures are the safest.' Despite his experience of King Ferdinando's incompetence he encouraged his disastrous foray into the Papal States, now the Roman Republic. All too soon the royal family had to escape to Sicily under Nelson's protection.

'Old, shrivelled, a piece of walking *verd antique*', as his crony the Earl-Bishop of Derry described him, Hamilton at sixty-nine was doomed to face ridicule while his wife flaunted her conquest of the infatuated hero. Sir William behaved with diplomatic dignity: he pretended not to notice. But he was mortified when he was recalled in January 1800 and Arthur Paget, his young successor, arrived in Palermo. The Queen begged her husband to apply for Hamilton's retention, but he was as tired of Emma's intrigues as of his wife's and he was none too sorry when they all departed together, the Queen, her son Leopoldo, three Princesses (future Queens), the Hamiltons, with Emma's mother Mrs Cadogan, and Miss Cornelia Knight, who described their journey to Vienna in her autobiography.

Hamilton's remaining years were spent as the least prominent member of a conspicuous trio on a series of triumphal tours. Since she had been Maria Carolina's confidante Emma had grown stouter, louder, and more lavish in every way. Nelson idealized her; his own wife was deserted and forgotten. While Hamilton longed for *otium cum dignitate* Emma wanted an audience of worldlings with whom he had little in common. He sought refuge with the Royal Society, the Society of Antiquaries, in the British Museum and in sale rooms. For his thirty-seven years as ambassador he received an inadequate pension of £1,200 per annum, and his negotiations for the payment of his extraordinary expenses in Palermo were as fruitless as they were humiliating. The recovery of his pictures and several cases of vases on board the *Foudroyant* were some consolation for the loss of his treasures in the wreck of the *Colossus*. The pictures were sold profitably at Christie's, the vases to his fellow antiquarian Thomas Hope. Together with Nelson he was awarded the honorary degree of a Doctor of Civil Law at Oxford, and wherever the trio went crowds gathered to cheer. But Sir William travelled without Emma to his estates in Wales, and without her he went fishing in the Thames. Like Sir Henry Wotton at Eton he became an enthusiastic angler, but he had no Izaak Walton to reminisce with when his thoughts returned to the fireworks of Vesuvius, the royal hunts near Caserta, the orange groves beside the glorious bay. His living work of art had expanded: Romney's nymph had become a blowsy Rubens. But Nelson remained under her spell until he was killed at Trafalgar.

After his decades in southern Italy the English winters were too severe for Hamilton's constitution. On 6 April 1803, at the age of seventy-three, he died in Emma's arms with Nelson holding his hand.

In the same year another ambassador of Scottish blood, Thomas Bruce, the seventh Earl of Elgin, stopped at Athens to inspect two hundred chests full of marble sculptures from the Parthenon and other parts of the Acropolis, leaving another Hamilton to supervise their shipping to England. On Sir William's advice he had hired the Neapolitan artist Lusieri and several draughtsmen to copy and record them in 1800. Their ultimate effect on the history of taste cannot be overestimated. Canova marvelled at their 'truth to nature united with the selection of ideal forms,' and Fuseli exclaimed about them: 'The Greeks were gods, the Greeks were gods!'

In this limited space I have been able only to sketch the salient features of the three ambassadors I have chosen for their influence on Anglo-Italian culture. Sir Henry Wotton, whose missions to the Venetian Republic were shorter than those of Mann to Florence and Hamilton to Naples, was the most Italianate. He never quite relinquished the rôle of Ottavio Baldi, and as Provost of Eton he instilled a love of Italian art and

A COGNOCENTI contemplating y̆ᵉ Beauties of y̆ᵉ Antique.

47 James Gillray's caricature of Sir William Hamilton.

literature into the gilded youth of England. The vast view of Venice which he presented to Eton still hangs in the College Hall.

Sir Horace Mann became so Florentine that he was never tempted to return to England: in that respect he too was Italianate. Sir William Hamilton's eclectic taste and hospitality gave him a European reputation among artists and scholars. Pryse Lockhart Gordon, a fellow Scot, wrote of him: 'he was a perfect Neapolitan both in mind and manners. ... He trafficked in the arts, and his hotel was a broker's shop. No one knew the value of a Greek vase or a gem better than the *cavaliere inglese*, or where to place it.' But he trafficked in the arts for a generous cause. As he wrote in his *Collection of Engravings from Ancient Vases*: 'My motive when I first began to collect this sort of Antiquity, was from the superior degree of merit I perceived in them with respect to the Fine Arts, and the profit I thought Modern Artists might reap from the study of them: a circumstance which did not seem to have been attended to sufficiently by former Collectors or Editors. I speak as a passionate lover of the Arts.'

Passionate lovers of the arts are rare among twentieth-century ambassadors, none of whom would be allowed to remain *en poste* like Hamilton for thirty-seven years, or like Mann for forty-eight. These represented a bygone civilization which, with all its defects, was more enlightened in matters of artistic taste.

LIST OF ILLUSTRATIONS

Engraving by David Loggan from
Cantabrigia Illustrata, Cambridge
1690
Eton College Library
Reproduced by permission of the
Provost and Fellows of Eton
College
Photo Eileen Tweedy

14 *M. T. Ciceronis de Officiis Libri III*,
1497
Eton Ms 149, fol. 1 r.
Given to Eton by Wotton
Eton College Library
Reproduced by permission of the
Provost and Fellows of Eton
College
Photo Eileen Tweedy

15 Letter from Wotton, dated 11
March 1619, written to the
Secretary of State, Sir Robert
Naunton
Eton Ms 188, letter 72
Eton College Library
Reproduced by permission of the
Provost and Fellows of Eton
College
Photo Eileen Tweedy

Sir Horace Mann (1706–86)

16 THOMAS PATCH (1725?–82)
*View of Florence from the Cascine
Gardens*
Canvas, 1771
Collection The Marquess of
Cholmondeley

17 JOHN ASTLEY (1730–87)
Portrait of Sir Horace Mann
Canvas, 1752
Made for Horace Walpole
Courtesy of The Lewis Walpole
Library, Yale University

18 ROSALBA CARRIERA
(1675–1757)
Horace Walpole, 4th Earl of Orford
Pastel on paper, 1741
Collection The Marquess of
Cholmondeley

19 THOMAS PATCH
A Party at Sir Horace Mann's
Canvas, c. 1765
Courtesy of The Lewis Walpole
Library, Yale University

20 Casa Manetti, Via Santo Spirito,
Florence

21 THOMAS PATCH
A Gathering at the Casa Manetti
Canvas, c. 1760–75
Courtesy of The Lewis Walpole
Library, Yale University

22 *Meleager and Atalanta*
Engraving from Baron Philipp von
Stosch, *Gemmae Antiquae*,
Amsterdam 1724

23 Formerly attributed to
Domenichino but now attributed
to Sassoferrato
Madonna and Child
From *A Set of Prints Engraved after
the most Capital Paintings in the
Collection of Her Imperial Majesty the
Empress of Russia Lately in the
Possession of the Earl of Orford*, 1788
Formerly at Houghton Hall,
Norfolk, now in the Hermitage,
Leningrad

24 THOMAS PATCH
*A Gathering of Dilettanti round the
Medici Venus*
Canvas, c. 1760–70
Brinsley Ford Collection

25 JOHANN ZOFFANY (1734–1810)
*The 'Tribuna' of the Uffizi Gallery at
Florence*

Canvas, 1772–79
Reproduced by gracious permission
of Her Majesty the Queen
26 Detail from the *Tribuna*, showing
Sir Horace Mann and Thomas
Patch
27 Three figures from the Brancacci
Chapel, Santa Maria del Carmine,
Florence
From Thomas Patch, *Life of
Masaccio*, Florence 1770–72
28 Baptistery doors, Florence
From Thomas Patch and
Ferdinand Gregori, *Libro della
seconda e terza porta di bronzo della
chiesa di Giovanni Battista di Firenze*,
Florence 1774
29 ENRICO HUGFORD (1695–1771)
Rocky Landscape
Scagliola
Museo dell'Opificio delle Pietre
Dure, Florence
Photo Alinari-Brogi

Sir William Hamilton (1730–1803)

30 View of Naples
After a drawing by Pietro Fabris
from William Hamilton, *Campi
Phlegraei: Observations on the
Volcanos of the Two Sicilies*, Naples
1776–79
31 DAVID ALLAN (1744–96)
*Sir William Hamilton in the robes of a
Knight of the Bath*
Canvas, 1775
National Portrait Gallery, London
32 DAVID ALLAN
*Sir William and his first wife at
Naples*
Copper, 1770
Collection The Earl Cathcart

33 Attributed to Pietro Fabris (*fl.* 2nd
half 18th cent.)
*A room in the Palazzo Sessa with Sir
William Hamilton and Lord Fortrose*
Canvas, *c.* 1770
Property of Jocelyn Feilding Fine
Art Ltd
34 Attributed to Pietro Fabris
*A room in the Palazzo Sessa with Sir
William Hamilton, Lord Fortrose and
the violinist Pugnani*
Canvas, *c.* 1770
Property of Jocelyn Feilding Fine
Art Ltd
35 View of the eruption of Vesuvius,
9 August 1779
After a drawing by Pietro Fabris
from William Hamilton, *Campi
Phlegraei: Observations on the
Volcanos of the Two Sicilies*, Naples
1776–79
36 A night view of a current of lava,
11 May 1771, with Sir William
Hamilton and Their Sicilian
Majesties
After a drawing by Pietro Fabris
from William Hamilton, *Campi
Phlegraei: Observations on the
Volcanos of the Two Sicilies*, Naples
1776–79
37 View of the eruption of Vesuvius
on Sunday night, 8 August 1779
After a drawing by Pietro Fabris
from William Hamilton, *Campi
Phlegraei: Observations on the
Volcanos of the Two Sicilies*, Naples
1776–79
38 View of the first discovery of the
Temple of Isis at Pompeii
After a drawing by Pietro Fabris
from William Hamilton, *Campi
Phlegraei: Observations on the*

Volcanos of the Two Sicilies, Naples
1776–79

39 Frontispiece
From William Hamilton,
*Collection of Engravings from Ancient
Vases*, Naples 1791–95

40 Vase painting
From Pierre François Hugues,
*Collection of Etruscan, Greek and
Roman Antiquities from the Cabinet of
the Hon. W. Hamilton*, Naples
1766–67

41 Portland Vase
Roman glass, 1st cent. AD
British Museum, London

42 JOSHUA REYNOLDS (1723–92)
*A group of members of the Society of
Dilettanti*
Canvas, 1777–79
A meeting of the Society (2 March
1777) at which Sir William
Hamilton was introduced as a new
member
The Society of Dilettanti

43 GEORGE ROMNEY (1734–1802)
Lady Hamilton as Circe
Canvas (unfinished), *c.* 1782

Tate Gallery, London

44 One of Lady Hamilton's
'Attitudes'
Engraving by Thomas Piroli from
Frederick Rehberg, *Drawings
faithfully copied from nature at Naples
and with permission dedicated to the
Right Honourable Sir William
Hamilton*, 1797

45 L. F. ABBOT (1760–1803)
Horatio Nelson
Canvas, *c.* 1800
National Maritime Museum,
Greenwich

46 FILIPPO TAGLIOLINI (?–1812)
Queen Maria Carolina
Naples biscuit ware, Real Fabbrica
Museo di Capodimonte, Naples
Photo Soprintendenza ai Beni
Artistici e Storici, Naples

47 JAMES GILLRAY (1756–1815)
*A Cognocenti contemplating ye
Beauties of ye Antique*
Caricature of Sir William
Hamilton
Etching, 1801
British Museum, London